Presented to:

....

By:

....

Date:

....

PLACE
A PHOTO OF
YOUR CHILD
HERE

"The words
of the Lord are perfect...
they are more precious than gold...
they are sweeter than honey...
in keeping them there is
great reward!"

PSALM 19:7-11

THE First Step BIBLE

BY MACK THOMAS

ILLUSTRATED BY JOE STITES

Gold 'n' Honey

BOOKS

THE FIRST STEP BIBLE

© 1994 by Questar Publishers, Inc.
Illustrations ©1994 by Joe D. Stites, All Rights Reserved

International Standard Book Number: 0-310-70136-8

Printed in the United States of America

THE FIRST STEP BIBLE was previously published by
Gold and Honey, a division of Multnomah Publishers.

For information contact

Zondervan Publishing House

Grand Rapids, Michigan

01 02 03 04 05 – 15 14 13 12 11 10

Contents

Old Testament Stories

I See What God Made

My name is Adam. What do I see?
I see the bright sunshine God made.
And God says, "It is good!"

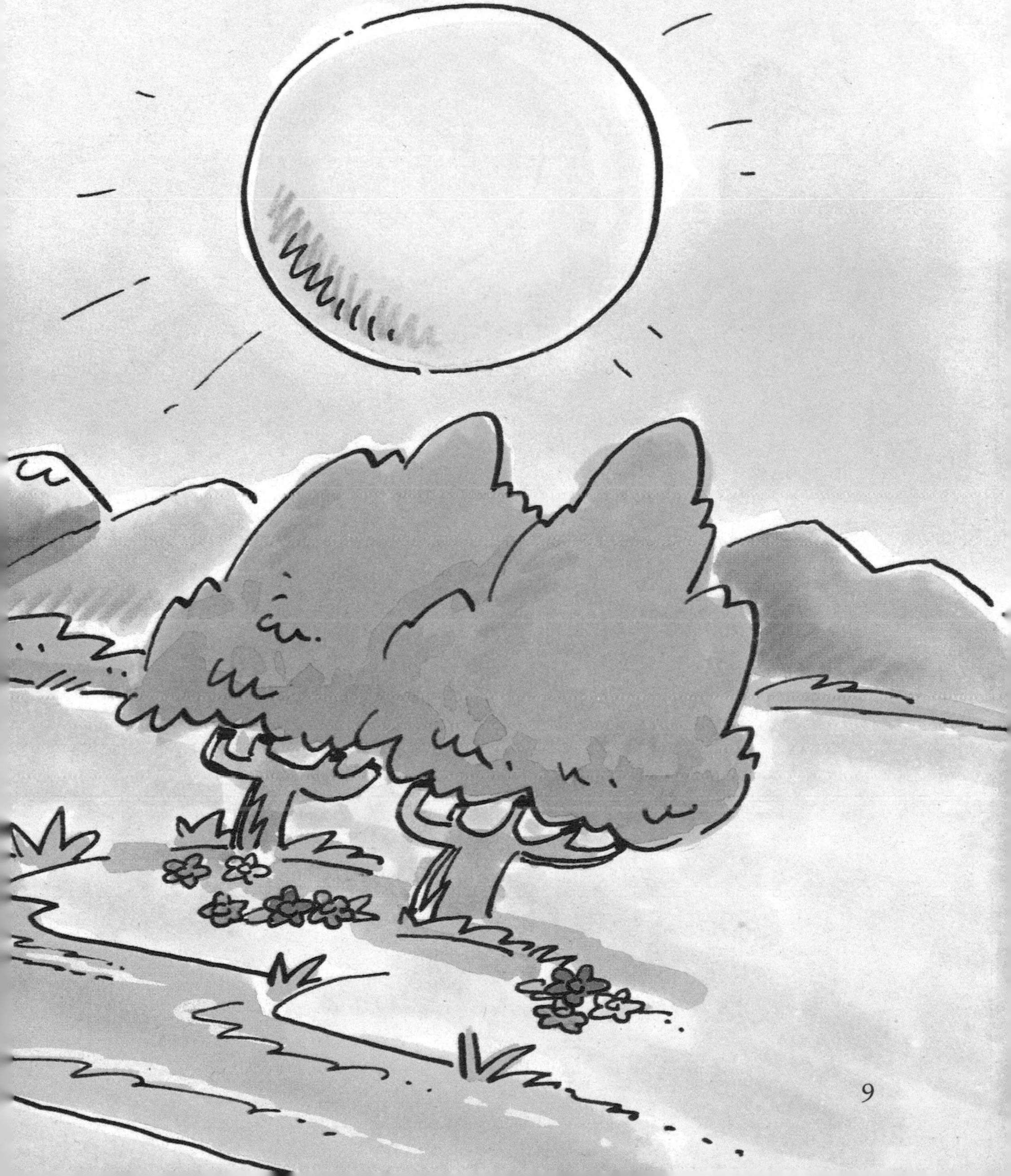

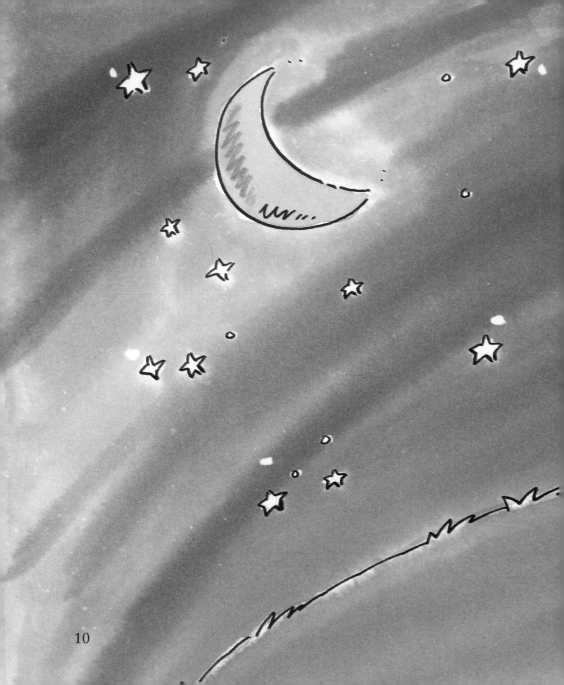

I see the moon and the stars God made.
And God says, "They are good!"

I see the flowers and the trees God made.
And God says, "They are good!"

I see the fish and the birds God made.
And God says, "They are good!"

I see my animal friends God made.
And God says, "They are good!"

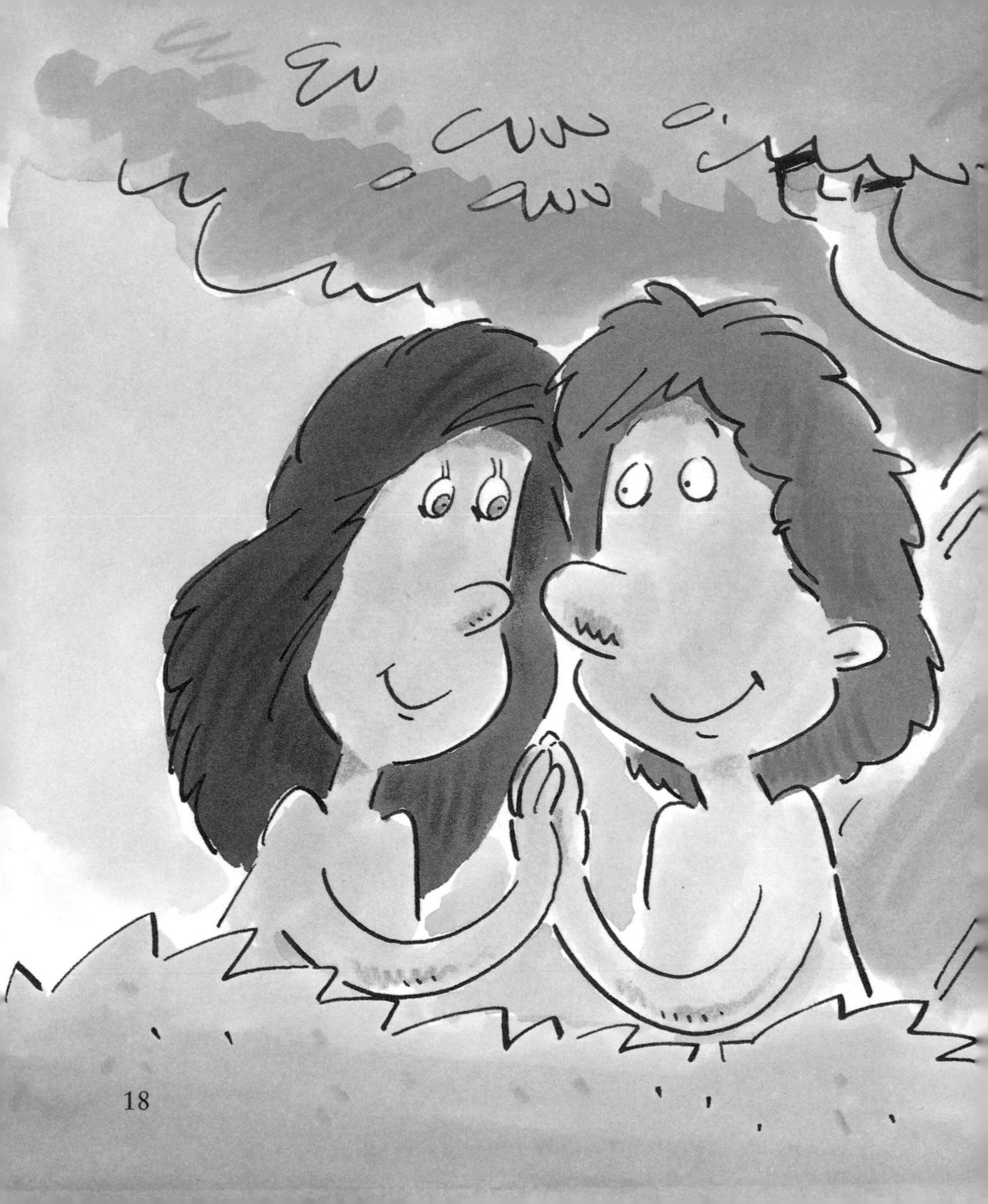

I see Eve, the woman God made…

I even see the ME God made!
And God says, "This is all VERY GOOD!"

God made you, and God made me,
and so many good things for us to see!

Where Is the Water?

Hello! My name is Noah.
I heard God say,
"Build a BIG BOAT, Noah."
So I am building a BIG BOAT.

But where is the water for the boat to ride on?
"The water is coming," God says.

Now the boat is ready.
Little animals come to get inside the boat.
But where is the water?

The water is coming!

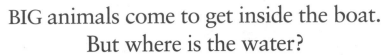

BIG animals come to get inside the boat.
But where is the water?

The water is coming!

My family comes to get inside the boat.
But where is the water?
The water is coming!

God closes the door so we will be safe.

31

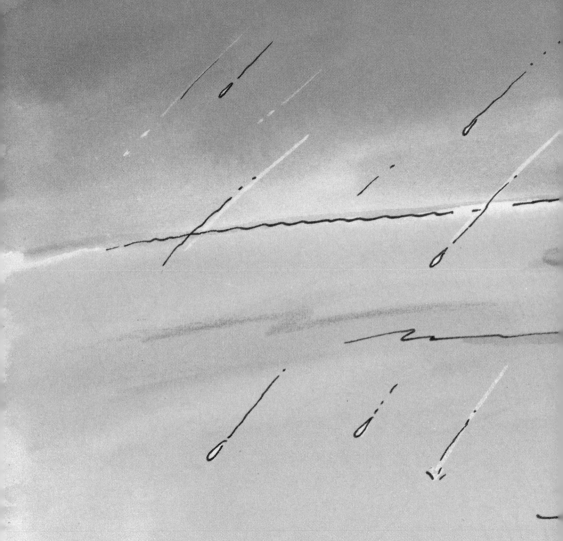

And HERE comes the WATER!
Water everywhere!

Inside the boat God keeps us safe...

until the day the water is gone. Then God says,
"Come out, everyone, come out!"
And we are so glad God keeps us safe!

Our Own Little Baby

My name is Abraham.
Sarah is my wife.
We have cows. We have sheep.
But we don't have our own little baby.

God says, "I will show you a new place
where you can live."

In this new place we have more cows.
We have more sheep.
But we don't have our own little baby.

Tonight God says,
"Look in the sky, Abraham!

Can you see all the many, many stars?
And you will have many, many children."

43

Then God says,
"Very soon I will give you a little baby boy."
And will God do it?

YES! This is our new baby boy.
And oh, how much I love him!
He is a present from God!

Stairs to Heaven

Hi! My name is Jacob.
I am on a long, long trip all by myself.
The sun is going down, and I am so tired.
Where will I sleep?

I will sleep on the ground.
A rock will be my pillow.
Good night!

While I sleep, I dream about stairs.
The stairs go all the way up to heaven,
all the way up to God.
Angels go up and down the stairs,
up and down, up and down.

I hear God say, "Jacob,
I will take care of you on your long, long trip.
Then you will come home safe."

What a good morning after such a good night!
I will not forget about the stairs to heaven.

I will always look and see
how God takes care of me!

My name is Joseph.
Look in my hands. What do you see?
This is *grain*.
We need this grain to make our bread—
good bread to eat. *Mmmmm!*

Today, everyone has so much grain.
So much grain to make so much bread.
We do not need this much—not now.
What should we do?

61

I know what to do,
because God tells me.
I say, "Come this way, everyone!
We can keep some grain right here.
We can save it."

Oh, look! What has happened now?
All the food is gone.
No one has grain anymore.
No one can make bread anymore.
Soon everyone will be hungry.
What should we do?

I know what to do,
because God tells me.
I say, "Come this way, everyone!
Right here is the grain we saved.
Take this grain, and make more bread.

When God tells me what to do,
I listen. And everyone is glad.

The Baby in the Basket

My name is Miriam.
I have a little baby brother.
A bad king wants to hurt my baby brother.
What should we do?

My mother makes a little basket-boat.
She puts my baby brother in the basket.
She hides the basket in the river.

I wait and I watch.
I want to see what will happen next.

Oh! Here comes a princess!

She sees the basket.
And she sees the baby.

My baby brother cries:
Waaaaa! Waaaaa!

I say to the princess,
"Would you like someone to help you
take care of that baby?"

"Yes," the princess answers.

My mother and I help the princess
take care of my baby brother.

Then the princess says,
"I found this baby in the river,
and I will name him Moses."

How Will We Cross the Water?

Hi! My name is Moses.
I am not a baby anymore.
I am with God's people.
God wants us to go away from a bad king.
God will take us to new homes far away.

But the bad king does not want us to go.
So God sends SO MANY frogs
to bother the king.

Then God sends SO MANY bugs.

Then God sends SO MANY grasshoppers.
Very soon, the bad king will let us go
to our new homes.

Now we can go! But our new homes
are far away. We need to cross all this water.
How can we cross the water?

Look how God helps us!
God moves the water out of our way!
Now we can keep going to our new homes.

And we are glad!

Hungry and Thirsty

Our new homes are still far away.
God's people say to me,
"Moses, there is no food here for us to eat.
We are TIRED and we are HUNGRY!"

99

So I pray to God.
And God says, "Tomorrow morning
you will find food all over the ground."

Then we all go to bed.
God's people go to sleep.
Good night!

Wake up! It's morning!
Look at the food all over the ground—
such good food for us to eat!

But now God's people say to me,
"Moses, there is no water
here for us to drink.
We are HOT and we are THIRSTY!"

107

So I pray to God. And God says,
"Water will come from that rock over there."

Look at the water—
good, cold water for us to drink!
God takes such good care of us!

Our New Homes

My name is Joshua.
God wants me to help His people.
Now we are ready to find our new homes.
Where will our new homes be?

Look! Our new homes will be across this river. Everything over there will belong to us.

But the river is full of water.
How will we cross the water?

Look how God helps us!
God moves the water out of our way!
Now we can go to our new homes.
And we are glad!

117

A Mighty Soldier

Hello! My name is Gideon.
God's people are living in new homes.
But bad people are hurting us.
Who will help us?

God's angel comes to me and says,
"YOU are a mighty soldier, Gideon!
YOU can help God's people!
God will make you strong!"

121

So I blow my trumpet — loud!
TA-TA-DAH! TA-TA-DAH! TA-TA-DAH!
And more soldiers come.
Together we help God's people.

God Hears My Prayer

My name is Hannah. I am crying
because I do not have a little baby.
So I pray to God: "Lord God,
please give me a little baby boy."
And will God do it?

125

YES! This is my new baby boy.
His name is Samuel.
He is a present from God!

Someone Calls My Name

Hi! My name is Samuel.
I am not a baby anymore.
I am a helper to this man Eli.
I help Eli when he prays to God.

Now it is bedtime. Good night!
Everything is dark.
Everything is quiet.

Oh, but listen! I hear something!
Someone is saying,

"SAMUEL! SAMUEL!"

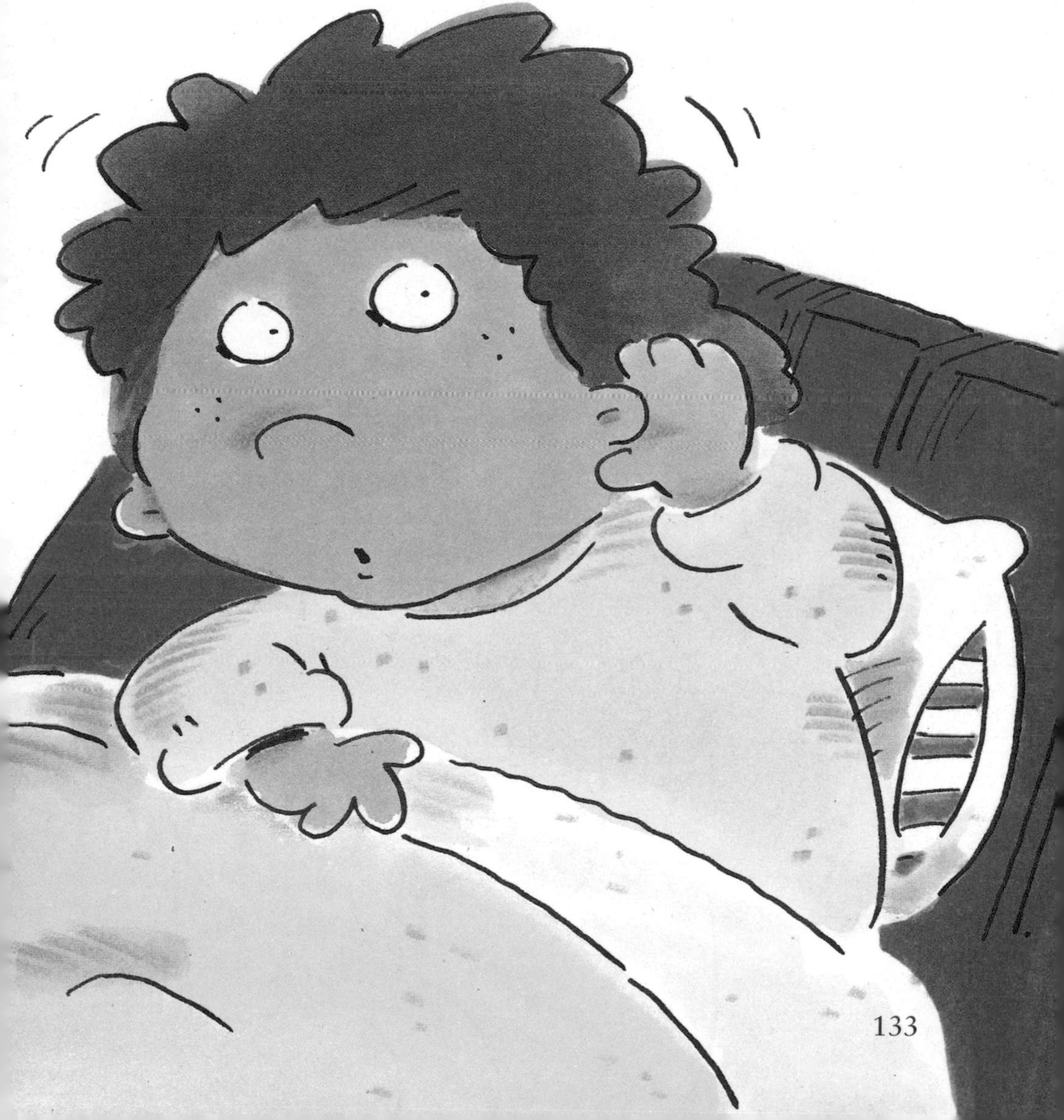

Here I am, Eli!
Eli wakes up and says, "But I did not call you.
Go back to bed, Samuel."

So I go back to bed.

But I hear something again!
Someone is saying,

"SAMUEL! SAMUEL!"

Here I am, Eli!
Eli wakes up and says, "But Samuel,
I did not call you. Please go back to bed."

So I go back to bed.

But I hear something again!
Someone says,

"SAMUEL! SAMUEL!"

This time Eli says,
"Samuel, GOD is calling you!
If you hear Him again, answer Him."

So I go back to bed.

I hear someone say,
"SAMUEL! SAMUEL!"

And I answer, "Yes, Lord God, I will listen
to whatever You tell me."
God tells me many things.
And I will do what God tells me to do.

Stronger than a Giant

Hello! My name is David.
I am a shepherd boy.
I take good care of sheep.

Sometimes a lion wants to hurt my sheep.
I will not let the lion hurt my sheep.
And God will not let the lion hurt me.

I like to sing.
I sing songs to God,
because God takes good care of me.

Today I have come to see my big brothers.
My big brothers are soldiers.
But all the soldiers are afraid.
Why are they afraid?

153

They are afraid of this giant!
This giant does not love God.
This giant wants to hurt God's people.

155

But God will not let this giant hurt me!

God makes me strong!
The giant comes down.
And God's people are not afraid anymore.

God keeps us safe. We are glad!
And I will always sing to God.

In a Secret Place

My name is Elijah. God brought me here
to this secret place. God will keep me safe.
But I have no food here.
What will I eat?

163

Look! God sends birds to bring me food:
bread and meat—so good to eat!

Thank You, God,
for taking such good care of me!

My name is Daniel.
I love God. And I pray to God,
because God is big and strong!

I eat food that is good for me.
Then God makes ME big and strong.
And I keep loving God.
And I keep praying to God.

But some people do not love God.
They do not want me to pray to God.
They throw me into a dark, dark place
full of LIONS.

Will the lions hurt me?

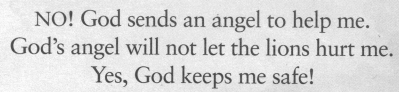

NO! God sends an angel to help me.
God's angel will not let the lions hurt me.
Yes, God keeps me safe!

New Testament Stories

My name is Mary.
Something is making me afraid.

178

Is it a stormy wind?
Is it a loud noise?
What could it be?

OH! It's someone bright with light—
an angel!

"Don't be afraid!" says the angel.
So I am not afraid anymore.

The angel says,
"God is happy with you.
God will give you a very special Baby."

The angel tells me the Baby's name.
Not Sammy. Not Danny.
Not Zack or Zeke.
Not Matthew, or Jimmy, or Pete.
No, the Baby's name will be…

Jesus!

189

Taking Good Care of Jesus

Hello! My name is Joseph.
Mary is my wife.

See Mary's new Baby Jesus!
Mary keeps Him covered, safe and warm.
And now He is asleep in a manger.

God tells me
to take good care of Mary and Baby Jesus.
So that is what I do.

KNOCK, KNOCK, KNOCK!
Oh, someone has come to see us.
Now who could that be?

Something Good to Tell You

Hello! I am a shepherd.
My friends are shepherds, too.
We take good care of sheep.
And we have something good to tell you.

199

Tonight we were putting our sheep to bed.
"Good night, sheep," we said.
"Go to sleep!"

And oh, the night was dark, SO dark.
Everything was still and quiet.
So still. So quiet. *Shhhh!*
Not a sound. Not a stir.
Then suddenly…

EVERYTHING was BRIGHT!
We saw an angel! And we were afraid.

"DON'T be afraid!" said the angel.
So we were not afraid anymore.

The angel said,
"I have something GOOD to tell you:
God's Son was born today!
Go see the special Baby.
He is covered, safe and warm.
He is sleeping in a manger."

Suddenly angels were everywhere,
singing happy songs to God!
Then they went away
so high up in the sky…

And we ran here to see the special Baby!

Follow the Star

We are Wise Men.
High in the sky we see a bright new star.
Do you see it too?

WHY is this star here?
Because a very special Baby has been born.
Let's take Him presents!

215

WHERE will we find the special Baby?
Let's follow the star!
The star will show us the way.

217

Far, far, far we go—
up hill…

219

down hill...

this way…

that way…

225

Look! Here is the star, and here we are!
And WHO will we find right under that star?

LOOK!
Here is the Baby Jesus!

Let's watch the Baby Jesus grow…

He grows so BIG
in every way.

233

He grows so STRONG,
to work and play.

He grows so TALL,
each new day.

And He knows how much
God loves Him!

*Do you know how much
God loves you?
Lots and lots and lots!*

Look for Someone Special

My name is John the Baptist.
My clothes are made from camel hair—
I wear what a camel wears!

For breakfast and lunch,
I like to have grasshoppers—
so munchy and crunchy to eat.
Mmmmm!

243

And for supper and snacks,
I like to eat honey—
a sweet, sweet treat.
Mmmmmm!

I don't live in a house like you.
I live outside in the rocks and the hills,
with the stars and the sky
and the wind.

Many, many people come out
to the rocks and the hills to see me.
And I tell them,

"Watch for Someone Special!
KEEP LOOKING!
He's coming!"

One day I say, "LOOK! He is here!"

Now WHO do you think has come?

Yes! Here is Jesus—
all grown up, so good and strong…
and He knows how much
God loves Him!

253

A Day with Jesus

Hi! My name is Andrew.
My friend and I see Jesus walking.
We want to be with Him.

We ask Jesus, "Where do you live?"

"Come and see," Jesus answers.
So we go with Jesus.

All day long we stay with Jesus.
We talk and we laugh and we pray,
until the sun goes away...

and the moon and the stars
come out to play.

Yes, there is nothing better
than spending a day with Jesus!

A Sick Little Boy

I am a soldier.
My little boy is sick. Oh, he is SO sick!
I am afraid he will NEVER get well.

I hurry away to find Someone.
Now WHO do you think
I want to find?

I find Jesus!
"Lord Jesus," I say,
"please make my little boy get well."

I hurry home.
And WHO do you think
I will see at my door?

I see my little boy!
Jesus made him well.

Hello! My name is Simon Peter.
Andrew is my brother.
This is our fishing boat.
Tonight, we are going fishing.

Out where the lake is deep,
we drop the net into the water. SPLASH!
Down, down, down goes the net.

We wait a little while.

Then we pull the net up, up, up.
Uh oh! No fish this time!

"Let's try it again," I say.
Down, down, down goes the net.

We wait a little while.

Then we pull the net up, up, up.

Uh oh! No fish this time!

We try it again.
Down, down, down goes the net.

We wait a little while.

Then we pull, pull, pull the net up.

Uh oh! No fish this time!

Oh, we are SO tired!
We fished all night long.

We want to go home and rest.
But first we listen to Jesus.
And Jesus says,

"Go back out
where the lake is deep.
Catch some fish with your net!"

So we take the boat out
where the lake is deep—
just because Jesus tells us to.
We drop the net down, down, down.

And we wait a little while.
Do YOU think we will catch any fish?

all because Jesus told us to!

Jesus Touched Me

Oh, look at me! I am sick.
Do you see my sore skin?
It hurts so much!

295

All day long my skin keeps hurting.
OUCH!

All night long my skin keeps hurting.
OUCH! OUCH!

The sores get worse and worse.

So I find Jesus. I say, "Lord Jesus, if You want to, You can make me well."

"I DO want to," Jesus tells me.
Jesus touches me.
I can feel His big, strong hand.
And He says, "Be well!"

Look at me, everybody!
My skin does not hurt anymore.

And YOU know why, don't you?
Because Jesus made me well.

Everywhere with Jesus

We are the disciples.
We go EVERYWHERE with Jesus.
We walk along the road with Him.

We climb a mountain with Him.

And we stay close
when Jesus talks to so many people.

311

Tonight Jesus tells us,
"Let's go to the other side of this lake."

So we get into the boat with Jesus.
But soon the dark night becomes stormy.

The wind is blowing:
WHOOSH! WHOOSH! SWOOSH!

315

And water is jumping: SPLASH! SPLASH!
CRASH! Oh, we are so afraid!

But Jesus is not afraid. He is sleeping.
"Lord Jesus! Wake up!
Save us from this terrible storm!"

When Jesus wakes up, He says,
"Why are you so afraid?"

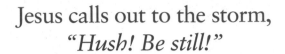

Jesus calls out to the storm,
"Hush! Be still!"

At once, the storm goes away.
Everything is quiet.
Everything is hushed.
Everything is still.

And we disciples say,
"Even the wind and the water do
whatever Jesus tells them!"

A Sick Little Girl

My name is Jairus.
My little girl is sick. Oh, she is SO sick!
I am afraid she will NEVER get well.

I hurry away to find Someone.
Now WHO do you think
I want to find?

I find Jesus!
"Lord Jesus," I say,
"please make my little girl get well."

So Jesus goes home with me.

As we get closer,
someone sad comes out of my house
and says, "Your little girl
will NEVER get well."

We see everyone crying. But Jesus tells me,

"Don't be afraid. Just listen to Me:
Your little girl WILL get well!"

Jesus goes into the house.

I hear Him say,
"Little girl, get up!"

And now,
WHO do you think I will see?

I see my little girl! Jesus made her well.
Jesus says, "She is hungry now.
Please give her something to eat."

My Little Lunch

I am just a little boy
with just a little lunch.
I have listened to Jesus all day long.
And now I am hungry!

I look all around me:
SO MANY PEOPLE!
They have listened to Jesus all day long.
Jesus says they are hungry, too.
He says they have no food—
nothing at all to eat.

So I say, "I will share my little lunch!"
The disciples take my lunch to Jesus.

Jesus looks up. He prays to God:
"Thank You, Father,
for this good food."

Then He gives my lunch
to all those hungry people.
But will my little lunch be enough?

YES!
Jesus makes my little lunch
into SO MUCH FOOD
for SO MANY PEOPLE!

And no one is hungry anymore.

I Could Not Hear

For such a long time my ears have been sick.
They are all closed up.
I cannot hear anything.

Birds might be singing.
Chirp! Chirp! Chatter!
But I cannot hear them.

Raindrops might be falling.
Pitter! Patter! Splatter!
But I cannot hear them.

Children might be laughing and playing.
But what does it matter?
I cannot hear them.

I cannot hear ANYTHING!

359

Then one day...Jesus comes.
Jesus touches my ears.

And YES—now I can HEAR!
I hear everyone shouting, "Jesus is SO good!"

Come Close, Little Ones

We are little children—
and we want to see Jesus.
But BIG PEOPLE are crowded all around Him.

Then we hear Jesus say…

"Come close, little ones!"
Jesus takes us in His arms.
He gives us such a hug
and such a smile!

And He says...

"Heaven belongs to children
just like YOU!"

Inside a Dark, Dark Place

My name is Lazarus.
I am in a dark, dark place.
I can never see again.
I can never hear again.

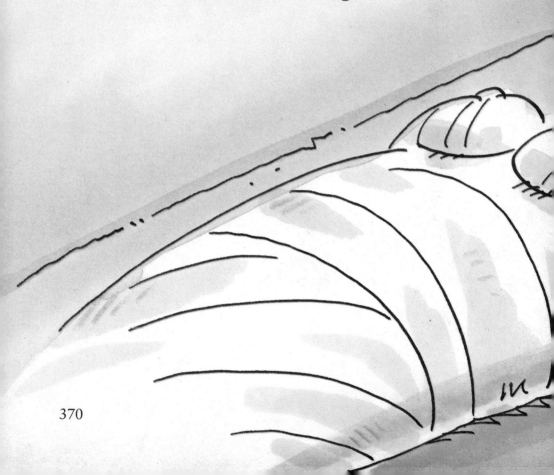

OH! But listen! I hear something!
Someone is saying,
"LAZARUS! COME OUT!"

So slowly I get up.
And slowly I walk out
of that dark, dark place.
And WHO do I see reaching out to me?

YES! My best friend Jesus!
Jesus calls us out of the dark, dark place.
He brings us into the light!

Jesus in My House

My name is Zacchaeus. I am small.
But everyone in front of me is SO TALL!
I cannot see Jesus.

So I run, run, run
to a tree beside the road.

I climb, climb, climb so high.

And I wait, wait, wait
for Jesus to walk this way.

HERE HE IS!
I can see Jesus now.
And He can see ME
high up in my tree.

Jesus says, "Hurry down, Zacchaeus!
I will stay at *your* house today."

So down I come.

And I tell Jesus,
"I am so glad You came to my house today!"

I Could Not See

For such a long time
my eyes have been sick.
They are all dark.
I cannot see anything.

A rainbow might be shining in the clouds.
But I cannot see it.

A flower might be growing by the road.
But I cannot see it.

The moon might be shining in the night.
But I cannot see it.

I cannot see ANYTHING!

Then one day…Jesus comes.
"Jesus, please HELP me!" I cry.

Jesus calls me close. He says,
"What do you want Me to do for you?"

Jesus touches my eyes.

And YES—now I can SEE!
I can see JESUS!
And I will stay close to Jesus
so I can see Him again and again!

Everybody, LOOK!
Here comes Jesus.
He is riding a little donkey.

Jesus is our King!
So we shout and sing: *Hosanna! Hosanna!*
Hosanna to the King!

Then we hear someone say,
"Jesus, these people are too loud!"

409

But Jesus answers,
"This is the singing that cannot be quiet!"

Hi! My name is John.
Come follow me up these stairs!

Do you see the big dinner?
Peter and I are getting everything ready.
Jesus will eat this dinner
with His special friends.

Here comes everyone now!
First comes Jesus.
"Hello, Jesus!"

And here are His disciples,
His special friends.
"Hello, disciples!"

But look at their dirty feet!

Everyone starts eating the big dinner.
Then Jesus gets up from the table.

He gets a towel.
He gets a big bowl full of water.

And He washes all those dirty feet!
Jesus loves His friends! He likes to help them.
He likes to help you and me.

My name is Mary Magdalene.
This morning I am so sad.
Some bad people hurt Jesus
and put Him in a dark, dark place.

Here is the dark, dark place.
I look inside.

Jesus is not here!
Where can He be?

I cry, and I cry, and I cry.
Then I hear someone say,
"Why are you crying?"
And when I look up...

And Jesus says, "Mary,
go tell My disciples
that I will soon go up to Heaven."

I hurry and find the disciples. I tell them,
"This morning I saw Jesus!
And He will never be
in that dark, dark place again!"

High on a mountaintop,
we disciples are with Jesus.
And Jesus says…

"Everywhere you go,
tell everyone you see
all about ME!"

Then Jesus goes up, up, up
high into the sky—
all the way up to heaven…
all the way up to God.

But don't be sad.
Someday Jesus will come back—
Oh yes! He will!
He will come back in the sky.
And you and I will see Him—
OH YES! WE WILL!

Tips for Parents

Teaching the Bible to the Very Young

Whether you're reading to your child from a full-text Bible or from a Bible storybook such as *The First Step Bible,* here are good things to remember:

◆ BE CONFIDENT that you're taking a wise step in introducing your child to the Bible. This book has universal appeal and value to young children: unique and dramatic stories... strong, authoritative presentations of right and wrong... and the inescapable message of God's character and love. By reading Bible stories aloud, you're pointing your child to a lifelong source of security, wisdom, and encouragement.

◆ Be ready to reread many stories again and again and again. Young children love repetition — they're thrilled to recognize something they've heard before, and feel proud of themselves for recognizing it. Give your child many opportunities to enjoy that feeling!

   After you've enjoyed several stories together, you may want to let your child begin choosing each time which story to read. Be a hero to your child by showing great delight in his or her favorites!

◆ FOCUS ON FUN! Try lots of changes in the volume and tone of your voice. You won't get bored reading a story for the twentieth time if each time you try saying the words with a little different stress and flavor, constantly improving your "delivery."

◆ Don't be shy about clearly showing the emotions appropriate to each story. As you read, be childlike yourself in easily exhibiting wonder, concern, relief, fear, and so on.

◆ Welcome your child's questions or comments. Think of Bible reading time not as an informational or entertaining time, but as a few moments of personal conversation between you, your child, and God.

◆ As you observe your child's responses to the Bible, ask questions and add your own comments. Establish the habit in your home of talking about the Bible and enjoying it together.

◆ Finally, be consciously aware of the Bible's powerful uniqueness. It isn't the only worthwhile book to read to children, but it has unequaled value for your child's intellectual, moral, and spiritual development. You would never limit your child's physical diet to snacks and sweets. In the same way, your family's character and spiritual growth depends on a wholesome diet. There's no better "health food" than the Bible for our minds and hearts, regardless of our age!